Letts

Phonics Success

Age 6-7

Phonics

Practice Workbook

Practice Workbook

Louis Fidge and Christine Moorcroft

Contents

Contents

Introduction

What is phonics?

Phonics is the relationship between sounds (phonemes) and letters or groups of letters (graphemes). Learning phonics involves listening to sounds, recognising sounds, discriminating between sounds, and learning how sounds are represented by letters.

Phonics Practice Workbook is based on current practice in schools and presents letters and sounds in ways that should be familiar to children from their school work. This book will support parents and carers in helping children to improve their reading and spelling using phonics.

Phonics for children (ages 6 to 7)

Children can use phonics to help them to read words they do not know. In fact, their phonic knowledge is sometimes tested in this way - reading 'pseudo' words using phonics alone. However, when children encounter words in a piece of text the context helps. This is useful when they are faced with words that could be pronounced in more than one way. Parents are encouraged to explain any new words in order to develop their child's vocabulary.

This book builds on children's previous learning (see *Phonics Practice Workbook Age 5–6*). It introduces a number of new sounds and the letters that can represent them, including…

- different ways of spelling sounds children have already learned
- alternative pronunciations for letters or combinations of letters
- adding prefixes to change the meanings of words
- adding suffixes to form plurals, past tenses and different forms of adjectives and verbs.

In addition to learning phonics, children should have opportunities to read as many different types of text as possible for pleasure and for information, as well as reading texts that warn or advise. Children should have opportunities to explore sounds and make up rhymes – however silly!

This book helps children to learn the relationship between sounds and letters. They will learn:

- Alternative spellings for vowel sounds, including those that are spelled using more than one letter.
- Alternative spellings for consonant sounds, including unusual ones such as gh for 'f' and sc or st for 's'.
- Different sounds represented by the same letters.
- Adding suffixes to change the meanings of words and the different sounds produced by the suffix -ed.
- Adding prefixes to change the meanings of words.
- Spelling strategies for difficult words.

How this book is organised

Spelling vowel sounds (pages 6–31) further develops children's knowledge of the different ways of spelling vowel sounds: 'ay' (ai, ay, eigh), 'igh' (y, igh, i–e, ie), 'oo' (oo, ew, u–e), 'oh' (oa, ow, o–e, oe), 'ow' (ow, ou), 'uh' (er, our), 'ar' (a, al), 'ee' (y, ey, ee, ea), 'or' (aw, au, or, oar), 'oy' (oi, oy), 'air' (air, are), 'ur' (ur, ear, or).

Spelling consonant sounds (pages 32–43) further develops children's knowledge of the different ways of spelling consonant sounds: 'ch' (ch, tch, t), 'l' (l, le), 's' (st, sc), 'sh' (ch, ci, ti, ssi), 'z' (z, s), 'f' (gh).

Suffixes (pages 44–79) helps to develop an understanding of how suffixes change the meanings and spellings of words. This section helps develop an understanding of spelling patterns for words where suffixes are added: -ed, -s, -es, -er, -est, -ful, -ly, -y.

Prefixes (pages 80–85) introduces simple prefixes that change the spelling and meaning of a word: un-, dis-, re-.

Spelling strategies (pages 86–94) helps children develop strategies to help them make the correct choices for spelling difficult words:
- Splitting longer words into syllables
- Noticing spelling patterns such as 'ould' in would and could
- Combining words to create compound words
- Using clues to help with difficult words such as friend, busy, cupboard
- Using quirky or funny mnemonics to help children remember tricky words such as beauty, equal, cycle.

What have I learned?

This section provides activities to help you and your child assess what has been learned. It helps you to determine what further practice your child needs. Consult your child's teacher if you have any concerns.

Sounds like ay

tray

tray

chain

chain

gate

gate

Read the rhyme

Colour the letters that say **ay**:   ay   ai   a-e

Today it may rain

So I shall take the train.

There was no long wait

So I shall not be late.

Parent's tip

Begin by reading the rhyme to your child and asking him/her which sound they hear often. Ask your child to write the letters that stand for the 'ay' sound. Then show the pictures and words at the top of the page and read them aloud. Point out the different letters that can be used to write this sound. Your child could then follow the rhyme on the page as you read it with him/her.

Read and match the words

Read the words. Listen to the **ay** sound.
Look at the letters. Colour the letters that say **ay**.

clay   fail   place   make

spray   claim   faint   play

cane   raid   sail   shape

Match the words to the ones in the chart.
Write the words below.

🍽 **tray**	⛓ **chain**	🚪 **gate**
clay spray play sp	sail fail claim faint raid	cane place shape

Sounds like igh

sky

high

kite

Read the rhyme

Colour the letters that say **igh**: y   igh   i-e

If I could fly high up in the sky
Like a kite in the night.
I think I might fly
Right out of sight.

Parent's tip

Begin by reading the rhyme to your child and asking him/her which sound they hear often. Ask your child to write the letters that stand for the 'igh' sound. Then show the pictures and words at the top of the page and read them aloud. Point out the different letters that can be used to write this sound. Your child could then follow the rhyme on the page as you read it with him/her.

Read and match the words

Read the words. Listen to the **igh** sound.
Look at the letters. Colour the letters that say **igh**.

my thigh white

sigh bite why shy

bright

right cry mine time

Match the words to the ones in the chart.
Write the words below.

sky	high	kite

Sounds like oo

boot

chew

ruler

Read the rhyme

Colour the letters that say **oo**:   **oo**   **ew**   **u-e**

Jude flew to the moon.
Luke drew a spoon.

Bruno, in a bad mood,
threw some food.

But what about June?
She got her flute and
played a tune.

Read and match the words

Read the words. Listen to the **oo** sound.

Look at the letters. Colour the letters that say **oo**.

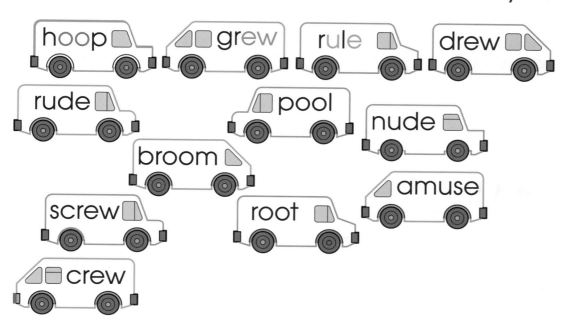

Match the words to the ones in the chart.

Write the words below.

boot	chew	ruler

Sounds like oh

road

blow

cone

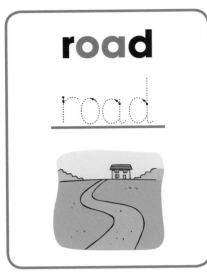

Read the rhyme

Colour the letters that say **oh**: oa   ow   o-e

I can row a boat.

I own a new coat.

I can score a goal.

I can mix in a bowl.

I am a mole.
I live in a hole.

Read and match the words

Read the words. Listen to the **oh** sound.

Look at the letters. Colour the letters that say **oh**.

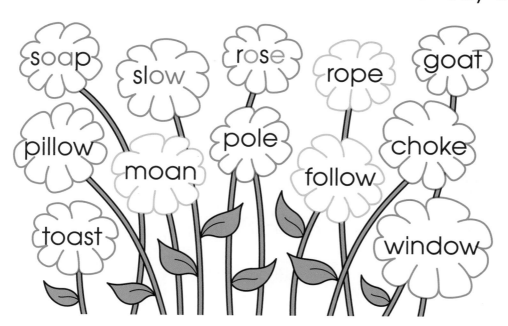

soap

slow

rose

rope

goat

pillow

pole

choke

moan

follow

toast

window

Match the words to the ones in the chart.

Write the words below.

road	blow	cone

Sounds like ow

Read the rhyme

Colour the letters that say **ow**:   **ow**   **ou**

The owl looked around
And came down to the ground.

The old white mouse
Came out of its house.

And a heavy shower
Soaked the flower.

Read and match the words

Read the words. Listen to the **ow** sound.
Look at the letters. Colour the letters that say **ow**.

now shout round town

about scowl found crowd

cloud house drown towel

Match the words to the ones in the chart.
Write the words below.

cow	mouse

Sounds like uh

hanger

hanger

armour

armour

Read the rhyme

Colour the letters that say **uh**: er   our

Mr Winner has his dinner.

It's not a dinner to make him thinner.

Lots of chips and fish in batter.

Is going to make him fatter.

He eats without a quaver

And says, "I love the flavour."

Read and match the words

Read the words. Listen to the **uh** sound.
Look at the letters. Colour the letters that say **uh**.

scatter colour favour batter

ladder harbour father paper

flavour winter neighbour letter

Match the words to the ones in the chart.
Write the words below.

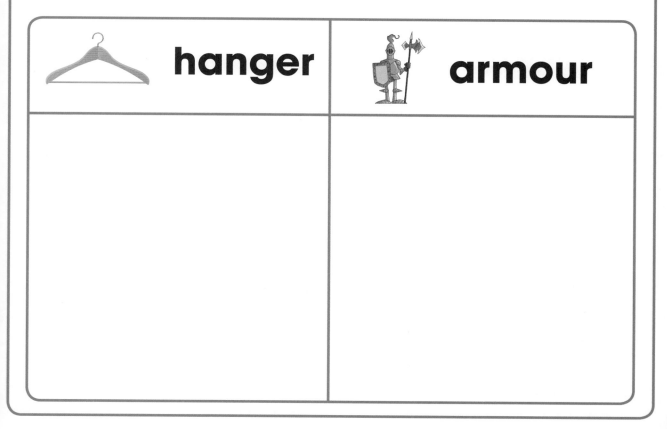

hanger	armour

Sounds like ar

shark

shark

palm

palm

Read the rhyme

Colour the letters that say **ar**:   **ar**   **al**

Martha sat under a palm
And put on some lip-balm.

Marge sailed her barge
And said, "I'm in charge!"

Read and match the words

Read the words. Listen to the **ar** sound.

Look at the letters. Colour the letters that say **ar**.

mark	calm	carpet	spark
calf	party	target	half
starve	calves	charming	parcel

Match the words to the ones in the chart.

Write the words below.

🦈 **shark**	🌴 **palm**

y or ey

cherry

cherry

barley

barley

Write the words

Read the words.

baby   money   key   honey   turkey   donkey

Write the words for the pictures.

_____

_____

_____

_____

_____

_____

Read and sort the words

Read the words. Colour **ee** or **ea**.

Sort the words into sets.

ee words	**ea** words

au or aw

sauce

sauce

claws

claws

Write the words

Read the words.

shawl laundry saucer jackdaw launch straw

Write the words for the pictures.

morning

morning

roar

roar

Write the words

Read the words.

oar storm whiteboard corn thorn chessboard

Write the words for the pictures.

_____

_____

_____

_____

_____

_____

Sounds like ay

reins

reins

hey

hey

Hey!

neigh

neigh

Neigh

Read the rhyme

Colour the letters that say **ay**:   ei   ey   eigh

Hey! Neighbours! Hey! Mr Grey!
Santa Claus is here on his sleigh!
Count the reindeer – one, two,
    three, four, five, six, seven, eight!
Pulling, pulling that heavy weight.

Parent's tip

Begin by reading the rhyme to your child and asking him/her which sound they hear often. Ask your child to write the letters that stand for the 'ay' sound. Then show the pictures and words at the top of the page and read them aloud. Point out the different letters that can be used to write this sound. Your child could then follow the rhyme on the page as you read it with him/her. After completing this page, return to p.6 and remind your child of the other letters that can be used to spell the 'ay' sound.

Read and match the words

Read the words. Listen to the **ay** sound.

Look at the letters. Colour the letters that say **ay**.

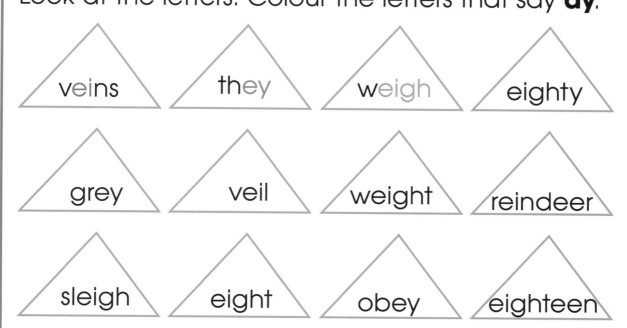

veins

they

weigh

eighty

grey

veil

weight

reindeer

sleigh

eight

obey

eighteen

Match the words to the ones in the chart.

Write the words below.

reins	hey	neigh

Words with ie

Make the words

Make some words with **ie**. Read the words.

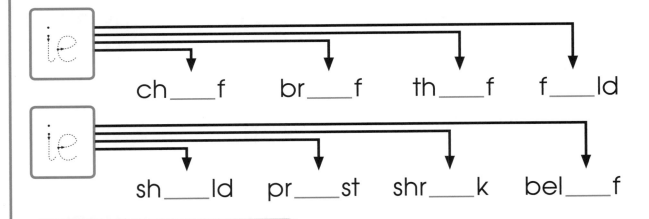

ch____f   br____f   th____f   f____ld

sh____ld   pr____st   shr____k   bel____f

Write the words

Write the words in the grid. Put one sound in each box.

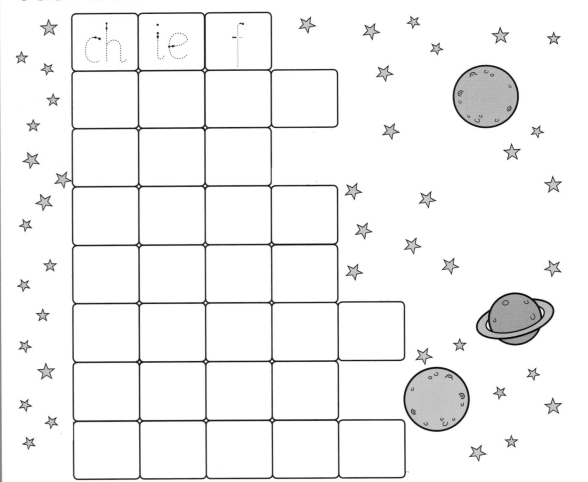

Make the words

Make some words with **oe**. Read the words.

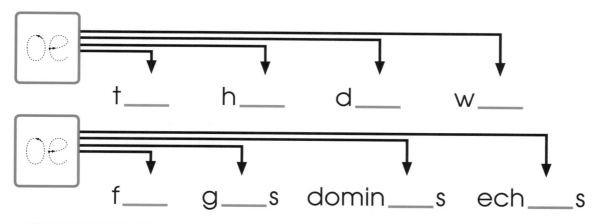

t____   h____   d____   w____

f____   g____s   domin____s   ech____s

Write the words

Write the words in the grid. Put one sound in each box.

oy or oi

oyster

oyster

oil can

oil can

Match the words

Read the words. Colour **oy** or **oi**. Match the words to their meanings.

soil	a Chinese sauce
boiler	money
enjoy	a small hoop
spoil	part of the ground/outdoors
coins	bothering or getting on your nerves
annoying	it heats water
quoit	to like doing something
soy	harm

Match the words

Read the words. Colour **air** or **are**. Match the words to their meanings.

airport	a dummy for scaring away birds
beware	get ready
software	left over
scarecrow	a place where planes take off and land
wheelchair	fix or mend
prepare	watch out
spare	a program for a computer
repair	a seat on wheels to help people get around

Sounds like ur

purse

Earth

world

Read the rhyme

Colour the letters that say **ur**: **ur   ear   or**
See if you can spot another set of letters that
say **ur**! Circle them.

The early bird catches the worm.
Here's a good one – nice and
firm.

To earn a worm I have to be
early.
Here's a nice one – fat and
curly.

**Parent's
tip**

Begin by reading the rhyme to your child and asking him/her which
sound they hear often. Ask your child to write the letters that stand
for the 'ur' sound. Then show the pictures and words at the top of the
page and read them aloud. Point out the different letters that can
be used to write this sound. Your child could then follow the rhyme on
the page as you read it with him/her. Remind your child of other
sounds: 'er' in German, Bért, perm; 'ir' in girl, third, circus. N.B. 'air' and
'are' represent a different sound but some regional pronunciations may
make them similar.

Read and match the words

Read the words. Listen to the **ur** sound.
Look at the letters. Colour the letters that say **ur**.

nurse	learn	word	burst

curve	worship	pearl	earn

worth	further	worst	search

Match the words to the ones in the chart.
Write the words below.

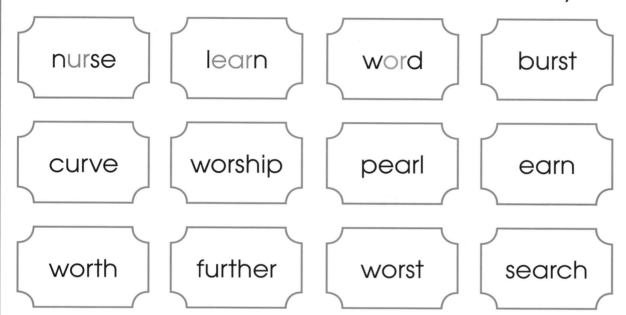

purse	Earth	world

Sounds like ch

cheese

match

picture

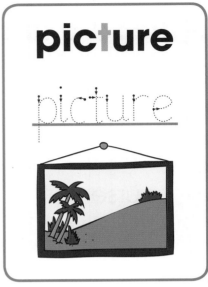

Read the rhyme

Colour the letters that say **ch**: **ch** **tch** **t**

The vulture is a greedy creature.

Its bald head is a natural feature.

It sits on a branch to watch for lunch.

Then snatches as much as it can to munch.

Read and match the words

Read the words. Listen to the **ch** sound.
Look at the letters. Colour the letters that say **ch**.

chicken   stitch   nature   fetch

mixture   peach   bench   butcher

capture   teacher   ditch   fracture

Match the words to the ones in the chart.
Write the words below.

🧀 **cheese**	╱ **match**	🖼 **picture**

When le says l

bottle

bottle

le

Read the rhyme

Circle **le** in the rhyme.

Mr Noble makes apple crumble

Mrs Noble likes to grumble,

"What a mess on my table! I wish you were able

To make a simple crumble without this jumble.

It's double the trouble when you make a crumble."

Write the words

Write the **le** words for the pictures. Circle **le** in the words.

kett____

jung____

buck____

pudd____

need____

tab____

ank____

eag____

puzz____

When st says s

whistle

whistle

st

Read the rhyme

Circle **st** in the rhyme.

Christmas shopping – jostle and hustle.
Away from the bustle,
Ice and snow glisten.

I listen
To paper rustle.

Match the words

Read the words. Colour **st**. Match the words to their meanings.

bristles	you do this with your ears
thistle	to close with buttons, laces or a zip
castle	a big strong house like a fort
whistle	part of a brush
wrestle	a spiky plant
nestle	to snuggle into a nest
listen	you blow it to make a noise
fasten	to fight in a contest

Sounds like sh

chef

chef

electrician

electrician

station

station

mission

mission

Read the rhyme

Colour the letters that say **sh**: **ch   ci   ti   ssi**

Charlotte the chef waits at the station.
Charlotte the chef is off on vacation.

"Is that your ticket?" asks an official,
"It's not real. It's artificial."

"It's real," says Charlotte with
passion.
Charlotte is ready for action.

Read and match the words

Read the words. Listen to the **sh** sound.
Look at the letters. Colour the letters that say **sh**.

Cherie   racial   action   percussion

session   Chantelle   Michelle   fraction

addition   special   Russian   social

Match the words to the ones in the chart.
Write the words below.

chef	electrician
station	**mission**

z or s

freeze

freeze

cheese

cheese

Read the rhyme

Colour the letters that say **z**: **z** or **s**

Joe's rose grows and grows
Because Joe sprays it with his hose.

"I'll win a prize
With a rose this size,"
Says Joe with his nose to the rose.

Read and match the words

Read the words. Listen to the **z** sound.
Look at the letters. Colour the letter that says **z**.

maze, please, easy, lazy, trousers, lizard, breeze, because, excuse, amazing, hazelnut, choose

Match the words to the ones in the chart.
Write the words below.

freeze	**cheese**

When gh says f

Make the words

Make some words where **gh** says f. Read the words.

trough

lau____   rou____

cou____   enou____

tou____   lau____ter

Write the words

Write the words in the grid. Put one sound in each box.

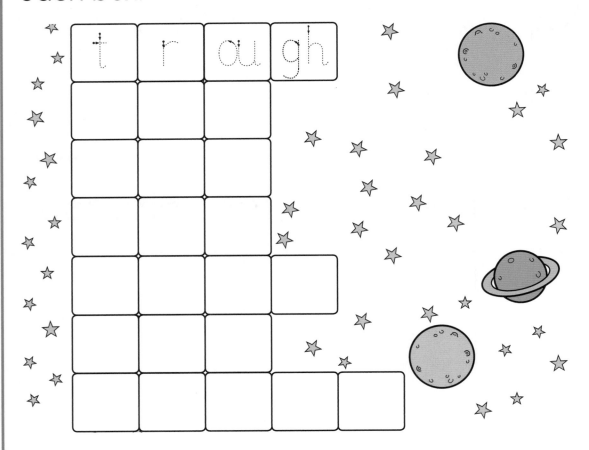

Make the words

Make some words with **sc**. Read the words.

____ene   ____ent   ____ience   mu____le

____issors   cre____ent   ____enery

Write the words

Write one of the words you made in each sentence.

 What a pretty ___scene___.

 The _____ery is lovely here.

 Tonight the shape of the moon is a _____.

 That's a strong _____.

 This _____ smells like roses.

 I am learning _____.

 We use _____ for cutting paper.

Read the words

Circle **-ed** in the words.

roasted

toasted

painted

fainted

bolted

jolted

Write the words

Add **-ed** to the end of each word.
Write the new word in the gap.

float

Yesterday I _floated_ in the pool.

act

Yesterday I _____ in a play.

boast

Yesterday I _____ about my work.

land

Yesterday I _____ on the moon.

mend

Yesterday I _____ the gate.

Suffix -ed (2)

splash → ed

Read the rhyme

Circle **-ed** in the rhyme.

I mixed it.

I fixed it.

I smashed it.

I crashed it.

I rowed it.

I mowed it.

Write the words

Add **-ed** to the end of each word.
Write the new word in the gap.

watch

Yesterday I _watched_ television.

pick

Yesterday I _____ some flowers.

row

Yesterday I _____ a boat.

jump

Yesterday I _____ over a wall.

help

Yesterday I _____ my mum.

Suffix -ed (3)

knit + t → ed
knitt → ed

knitted

Read the rhyme

Circle **-ed** in the rhyme.

I clipped it.

I snipped it.

I chopped it.

I dropped it.

I clapped.

I flapped.

Write the words

Add **-ed** to the end of each word.
Write the new word in the gap.

slip

Yesterday I _slipped_ on a banana skin.

whip

Yesterday I _____ some cream.

hum

Yesterday I _____ a tune.

hop

Yesterday I _____ along a line.

Suffix -ing (1)

play → ing

playing

Read the rhyme

Circle **-ing** in the rhyme.

I am rushing,

teeth need brushing,

lolly licking,

football kicking,

hiding, peeping,

now I'm sleeping!

Write the words

Add **-ing** to each word and write it under the picture.

bend	catch	cook	draw	jump
	sing	lift	pull	read

pulling

Suffix -ing (2)

ride → **ing**
rid → **ing**

riding

Read the words

Circle **-ing** in the words.

 wave – waving

 shave – shaving

 hide – hiding

 slide – sliding

 hose – hosing

 close – closing

Add -ing

Do these word sums with **-ing**. Remember to take off **e**. Write each word.

 write $+$ ing

writing

 smile $+$ ing

_____

 stroke $+$ ing

_____

 bake $+$ ing

_____

 dive $+$ ing

_____

 bite $+$ ing

_____

Take off -ing

Take **-ing** off each word. Put the **e** back.
Write the new word.

hoping	skating	taking
_____	_____	_____
wiping	joking	using
_____	_____	_____

Suffix –ing (3)

run + n → ing
runn → ing
running

i n g

Read the words

Circle **-ing** in the words.

 yap – yapping

 tap – tapping

 pin – pinning

 win – winning

 tug – tugging

 hug – hugging

Write the words

Add **-ing** to each word. Don't forget to double the last letter. Write the new word in the gap.

swim

I like _____.

skip

I like _____.

cut

I like _____.

dig

I like _____.

drum

I like _____.

nod

I like _____.

Suffix -s

Read the words

Circle **-s** in the words.

One toy, two boys.

One cat, two rats.

One rug, two bugs.

One man, two vans.

Write the words

Write the missing words.

One	Two
One cake	Two _cakes_
One kite	Two _____
One bone	Two _____
One nail	Two _____
One _tree_	Two trees
One _____	Two boats
One _____	Two clouds
One _____	Two mugs

Parent's tip

Read the first example with your child and ask, 'How do words change when they change from one thing to more than one?' (*Answer: Usually we add 's'.*) Ask your child to write the missing words and then read the words in the 'two' column aloud. Ask if the 's' at the end always says the same sound. (*Answer: No – sometimes it says 'ss' – as in boats, cakes, kites. At other times it says 'z' – as in mugs, trees, bones, clouds, nails.*)

Suffix -es

glass → es

glass glasses

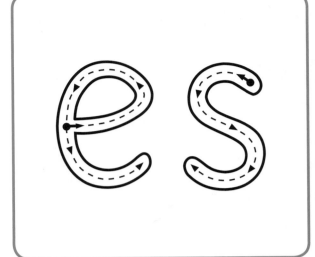

Read the words

Circle **-es** in the words.

one match

two matches

one patch

two patches

one box

two boxes

one fox

a family of foxes!

Write the words

Write the missing words.

One	Two
one brush	two _____
one box	two _____
one kiss	two _____
one watch	two _____
one _____	two dishes
one _____	two peaches
one _____	two arches
one _____	two sixes

Parent's tip

Remind your child how words change when they change from one thing to more than one. (*Reminder: Usually we add 's'.*) On a separate piece of paper, write 'wish' and ask your child to make it say more than one wish. Point out that 'wishs' is difficult to say, so words like this have 'es' added. After completing the page you could challenge your child to find and list other words that change in the same way. (You could also keep a list and make the challenge to list any words you haven't already thought of!)

Suffix -er (1)

fast → er

Read the words

Circle **-er** in the words.

I'm getting stronger.

I'm getting longer.

I'm getting taller.

I'm getting smaller.

I'm getting colder.

I'm getting older.

Add -er

Do these word sums with **-er**. Write each word.

[high] + [er]

_____

[low] + [er]

_____

[slow] + [er]

_____

[weak] + [er]

_____

[new] + [er]

_____

[bright] + [er]

_____

Take off -er

Take **-er** off each word. Write the new word.

neater	darker	lighter
_____	_____	_____

cooler	richer	poorer
_____	_____	_____

Suffix –er (2)

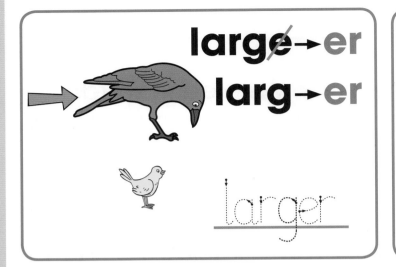

large → er

larg → er

larger

Read the words

Circle **-er** in the words.

gentle → gentler

loose → looser

wide → wider

ripe → riper

white → whiter

late → later

Add -er

Add **-er** to these words. Remember to take off **e**.
Write the new words.

fine _____   nice _____

brave _____   tame _____

simple _____   rare _____

Take off -er

Take **-er** off each word. Put the **e** back.
Write the new word.

later	wider	looser
_____	_____	_____

safer	fiercer	nicer
_____	_____	_____

Suffix -er (3)

 big + g → er
bigg → er

bigger

Read the words

Circle **-er** in the words.

getting wetter

getting hotter

getting thinner

getting fatter

getting fitter

getting sadder

Add -er

Add **-er** to these words. Remember to double the last letter.
Write the new words.

thin _____   flat _____

dim _____   mad _____

hot _____   trim _____

Take off -er

Take **-er** off each word. Don't forget to take off the letter that was doubled.
Write the new word.

bigger	wetter	hotter
_____	_____	_____

fatter	fitter	sadder
_____	_____	_____

Suffix –est (1)

fast → est

fastest

Read the sentences

Read the sentences. Circle **-est** in the words.

I'm the strongest.

I'm the longest.

I'm the tallest.

I'm the smallest

I'm the coldest.

I'm the oldest.

Add -est

Do these word sums with **-est**. Write each word.

high	+	est

_____

low	+	est

_____

slow	+	est

_____

weak	+	est

_____

new	+	est

_____

bright	+	est

_____

Take off -est

Take **-est** off each word. Write the new word.

neatest	darkest	lightest
_____	_____	_____

coolest	richest	poorest
_____	_____	_____

Suffix –est (2)

larg**e** → **est**
larg → **est**

largest

Read the words

Read the words. Circle **–est** in the words.

gentle → gentlest

loose → loosest

wide → widest

ripe → ripest

white → whitest

late → latest

Add -est

Add **-est** to these words. Remember to take off **e**. Write the new words.

fine _____

nice _____

brave _____

tame _____

simple _____

rare _____

Take off -est

Take **-est** off each word. Don't forget to put the **e** back. Write the new word.

latest	widest	loosest
_____	_____	_____

safest	fiercest	scarcest
_____	_____	_____

Suffix -est (3)

big + g → est
bigg → est

biggest

Read the words

Read the words. Circle **-est** in the words.

The wettest day.

The hottest day.

The thinnest worm

The fattest worm.

I'm the fittest.

The dimmest light.

Add -est

Add **-est** to these words. Remember to double the last letter. Write the new words.

thin _____   flat _____

dim _____   mad _____

hot _____   trim _____

Take off -est

Take **-est** off each word. Don't forget to take off the letter that was doubled. Write the new word.

biggest	wettest	hottest
_____	_____	_____

fattest	fittest	saddest
_____	_____	_____

Suffix -ful

care → ful

careful

f u l

Read the rhyme

Circle **-ful** in the rhyme.

As playful as a kitten.

As useful as a bee.

As powerful as a lion.

As cheerful as me!

Write the words

Find the words in the forest. Write the words.
Add **-ful** to the end of each word.

Suffix -ly (1)

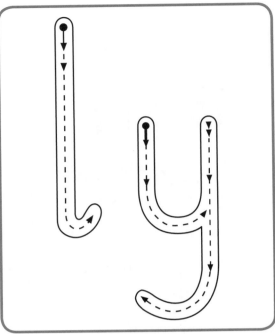

Read the words

Circle **-ly** in the words.

quickly

badly

rudely

sadly

Write the words

Add **-ly** to the words in the boxes.
Write these words in the gaps.
Read the sentences.

bright____	The sun shone _____ .
loud____	The lion roared _____ .
safe____	I crossed the road _____ .
fair____	I played the game _____ .
sad____	The girl cried _____ .
neat____	I always write _____ .
rude____	Some children speak _____ .
careful____	I always spell _____ .

Suffix -ly (2)

happy + i → ly

happi → ly

happily

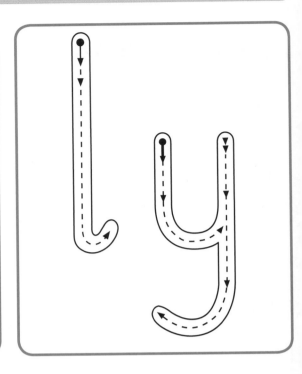

Read the words

Circle **-ly** in the words.

easily

noisily

merrily

angrily

Write the words

Add **-ly** to the words in the boxes.
Remember to change **y** to **i** first.
Write these words in the gaps.
Read the sentences.

cheeky_____	The girl spoke to the teacher _____.
nasty_____	The boy made fun of me _____.
clumsy_____	She knocked over the jug _____.
lucky_____	_____ I have a coat with me.
funny_____	_____ there were no children at school.
lazy_____	The cat stretched _____ _____.
creepy_____	The ghost slid into the room _____.
gloomy_____	"We're going to lose the match," he said _____.

Suffix -y

snow → y

snowy

ice → y
ic → y

icy

sun +n → y
sunn → y

sunny

Read the words

Read the weather forecast. Circle **-y** in the words.

It will be sunny here and shady there,

Squally, blustery, breezy, blowy – windy everywhere.

Snowy, icy, frosty and chilly

In places where it's hilly.

Hazy, misty, foggy and worst of all – smoggy.

Muddy here and showery there

Thundery, drizzly, choppy at sea – rainy everywhere.

Read and match the words

Read the words. Match the
-y words to the ones in the chart.
Write the **-y** words on the chart.

fizz → fizzy   taste → tasty   wobble → wobbly

spice → spicy   slop → sloppy   crunch → crunchy

chew → chewy   flake → flaky   grease → greasy

run → runny   salt → salty   crackle → crackly

snowy	**icy**	**sunny**

Prefix un-

un → lucky

unlucky

lucky   **unlucky**

Read the rhyme

Circle **un-** in the rhyme.

Pack your case for your holiday.

Unpack your things straight away.

It makes me happy to meet new friends.

But I am unhappy when my holiday ends.

Make the words

Make some words with **un-**.
Read the words you make.

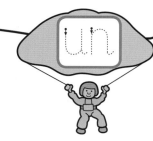

_____well
_____fair
_____even
_____happy
_____dress

_____cover
_____true
_____tie
_____load
_____block

Write words

Write the opposite of each word below.

uncover   cover   unhappy   _____
unload   _____   untie   _____
undress   _____   untrue   _____
unfair   _____   unwell   _____
unblock   _____   uneven   _____

Prefix dis-

dis → like

like

dislike

Read the rhyme

Circle **dis-** in the rhyme.

We are good when
we obey

but we're not good
when we disobey.

When Mum and Dad
appear,

like a flash we
disappear!

Make the words

Make some words with **dis-**. Write the words.

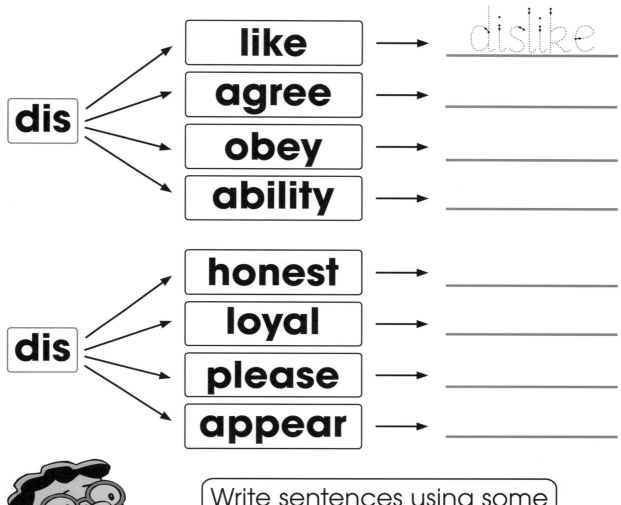

dis → like → _dislike_

agree → _____

obey → _____

ability → _____

dis → honest → _____

loyal → _____

please → _____

appear → _____

Write sentences using some of the words you made.

_____

_____

_____

Prefix re-

Shall I load the DVD again?

Yes. Please reload it.

re → load

reload

Write the words

Read the questions. Write the missing words in the answers. Use words with **re-**.
Circle **re-** in the words.

Will the shop open again?

Yes, it will

_____.

Shall I play that song again?

Yes, please

_____ it.

Make the words

Make some words with **re-**. Read the words.

re		re	
_____ set		_____ print	
_____ do		_____ place	
_____ write		_____ charge	
_____ new		_____ make	
_____ read		_____ cover	

Write the words

Write a word that means to do these again:

heat	_____	appear	_____
make	_____	boot	_____
check	_____	capture	_____
count	_____	dial	_____
fill	_____	fold	_____

Syllables

The children say their names. They clap for each beat.

Amy → **A** **my**

2 claps

James → **James**

1 clap

Write the numbers

Read the sentences. Write the number of claps for each name.

My name is Alice.	My name is Benjamin.
A | lice	Ben | ja | min
I clap _____ claps.	I clap _____ claps.
My name is Christopher.	My name is Sita.
Chris | to | pher	Si | ta
I clap _____ claps.	I clap _____ claps.

Match the words

Match the words that have 'look-alike', 'sound-alike' spellings.

Read the words.

would

borrow

carrot

feather

handle

parrot

worm

could

tomorrow

word

candle

heather

Parent's tip

Explain that sometimes it helps when spelling a tricky word if you know other words that are like it in some way. Show some examples, e.g:
- treasure/measure ('ea' and 's' might cause problems)
- heart/hearth ('ear' might be a problem)
- danger/ranger, but banger/clanger
- shoe/canoe

Compound words (1)

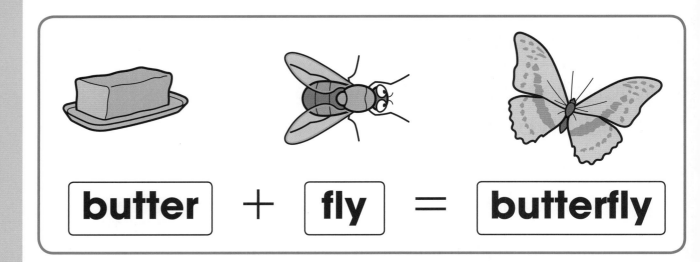

butter $+$ fly $=$ butterfly

Read the words

rainbow

rainfall

snowman

snowball

Word sums

Do these word sums. Write the answers.

tooth	+	brush	=	_____
bed	+	room	=	_____
wind	+	mill	=	_____
butter	+	cup	=	_____
star	+	light	=	_____
lady	+	bird	=	_____
sheep	+	dog	=	_____
hand	+	bag	=	_____
sun	+	shine	=	_____
book	+	mark	=	_____

Compound words (2)

| horse | + | shoe | = | horseshoe |

Read the rhyme

Worms are found **underground.**

Children run around in the **playground**.

It's nice and bright in the **sunlight**.

We all sleep tight in the **moonlight**.

Make the words

Make some compound words. Write the words.

hair	cake	
pan	day	
rain	cloth	
birth	brush →	hairbrush
table	bag	
book	bow	
hand	box	
letter	case	

Clues for tricky words

family

I am in my fam**i**ly.

shoe

The sh**oe** shone.

Read the sentences

Read the sentences.

There's a **g** in the si**g**n.

A **ball**oon is like a **ball**.

10

We of**ten** count to **ten**.

Parent's tip

Explain that some words have unusual spellings but that it sometimes helps if you use clues to help. Show the examples at the top of the page. It also helps if you learn the words by saying them as they are spelled. For example:

- cup – board
- fri – end
- of – ten (stressing the 'f' sound and the final syllable 'ten')
- sig – n.

This is sometimes called 'spell-speak'.

Write the words

Read the tricky words.
Cover the words. Write the words.

busy	across	friend
The bus is **bus**y.	There's a cross **a**cross the page.	**I** am your fri**end** to the **end**.
busy		
knee	office	cupboard
I bend my **k**nee to **k**ick.	There's **ice** in the off**ice**.	There's a **cup** on the **board** in the **cupboard**.

Remembering tricky words

Write the words

Read the tricky words and clues.
Write the words.

equal ????? **e**very **q**uestion mark **u**nder **a** **l**ine *equal*	beauty **b**ig **e**ars **a**re **u**seful **t**o **y**ou

cycle
 	
  can
 you
 circle
 legs
 easily
	laugh
	
	  look
	 at
	 ugly
	 gorillas
	 howling

Read the words and names.

Test 1

claim	slate	invite	flight
brewer	hollow	flavour	neighbour
charcoal	palm	honey	saucer

Test 2

board	freight	shield	believe
shriek	tomatoes	annoying	quoit
prepare	airline	dearth	world

Test 3

earthquake	satchel	hatchet	adventure
mixture	fetching	whistling	scrambled
racial	suction	station	lizard

What have I learned?

Read the words and names.

Test 4

enough	muscle	scissors	reported
diluted	tangled	clamped	stripped
treading	amusing	working	stalking

Test 5

calming	brewing	escaping	skidding
clutches	porches	birches	stranger
stronger	finer	fiercest	gentlest

Test 6

wonderful	awful	colourful	disgraceful
usually	unfairly	clumsily	nastily
unluckily	unwillingly	discovers	disobeyed

Test 7

disappearing	dishonest	recover	retrace
reappear	Christopher	featherweight	dragonfly
benchmark	busy	friend	cupboard